W9-BSW-647

The World's COOLEST Jobs

EXPLOSIVES EXPERT

Alix Wood

PowerKiD pres

New York

Published in 2014 by The Rosen Publishing Group, Inc.
29 East 21st Street, New York, NY 10010

Editor for Alix Wood Books: Eloise Macgregor
Designer: Alix Wood
US Editor: Joshua Shadowens
Researcher: Kevin Wood
Consultant: Paul Tierney, www.fireworks.co.uk

Photo Credits: cover, 5 bottom, 8, 9, 20, 21 © Defenseimagery.mil; 1, 4, 5 top, 6,
7 bottom, 11, 12 top, 13 top, 15 bottom, 16, 17 bottom, 18, 19, 23, 26, 27, 28 ©
Shutterstock; 15 top © Stanislav Tokarski/Shutterstock; 7 top © Andrew Davidhazy/
Rochester Institute of Technology/NASA; 10 © Antony Marcano; 13 bottom © Heptagon;
14 © Kenneth D. Durden/Dreamstime; 17 top © Timo Halén; 22 bottom © Lee Snider/
Dreamstime; 24 bottom, 25, 29 © Paul Tierney, www.fireworks.co.uk

Library of Congress Cataloging-in-Publication Data

Wood, Alix.
 Explosives expert / by Alix Wood.
    pages cm. — (The world's coolest jobs)
 Includes index.
 ISBN 978-1-4777-6011-6 (library) — ISBN 978-1-4777-6012-3 (pbk.) —
 ISBN 978-1-4777-6014-7 (6-pack)
 1. Explosives—Juvenile literature. 2. Pyrotechnics—Juvenile literature. 3. Vocational
guidance—Juvenile literature. I. Title.
 TP270.5.W66 2014
 662'.2—dc23

                                 2013023584

Manufactured in the United States of America

CPSIA Compliance Information: Batch #W14PK2: For Further Information contact Rosen Publishing, New York, New York at 1-800-237-9932

Contents

What Is an Explosives Expert?

Explosives experts work with explosives. Experts may defuse dangerous bombs. Some advise on the best blasting materials and techniques needed to **demolish** a building. They work anywhere explosives may be used, such as in construction, mining, on movies sets, and in the military.

There are different kinds of explosive experts. Explosive **technicians** handle powerful explosives such as those used in weapons or quarrying. **Pyrotechnicians** are responsible for handling and setting off **pyrotechnics**. Pyrotechnics are fireworks, explosions, flashes, smoke, and flames used in the entertainment industry. Many musical groups use pyrotechnics in their live shows.

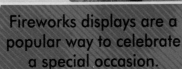

Fireworks displays are a popular way to celebrate a special occasion.

FACT FILE

An explosive is a substance that can be made to explode. Dynamite is a high explosive. It is used in mining, quarrying, construction, and demolition. Dynamite is made from an absorbent material such as sawdust soaked in **nitroglycerin.** The sawdust makes the nitroglycerin more **stable.** Dynamite is then wrapped in a protective coating. A blasting cap is placed on the top of the dynamite. The blasting cap creates a small explosion that triggers the larger explosion in the dynamite itself. A timer can be connected to the blasting cap.

blasting cap

sawdust

timer

dynamite

cooling tube

👍 THAT'S COOL

Bomb disposal experts dangerous job means they sometimes wear blast-resistant suits. The suits are hot in the desert. Some have cooling systems built into them. A network of tubes sewn into the suit are filled with water from a melting ice pack.

The Science of Explosives

Scientists design new explosives. Some explosives experts work with scientists to research new explosive materials and ways of working with them.

Explosives explode because they are made of materials that burn or break down very quickly, producing a lot of heat and gas. A typical explosive is made with some explosive material, a **detonator**, and an outer casing. The detonator causes a rapid **chemical reaction** in the explosive material. The explosive breaks down to form various **gases**. The energy from these gases becomes very hot and the gases expand quickly.

Gas forming after a chemical reaction

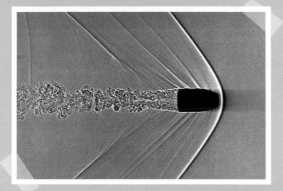

The curved line at the nose of this bullet is a shock wave. Other shock waves can be seen behind it.

Understanding how shock waves work can help explosives experts work out how to time each explosion. A shock wave is produced if a gas expands faster than the **speed of sound.** The explosion and the shock wave cracks the rock. Then the gas pressure formed after the shock wave fills and expands those cracks. The gas helps lift the rock away from the rock face.

Mining explosive experts knowledge of science helps them design explosives that break apart rocks into the exact size they need. Different rocks require different types of explosives. Granite needs a more powerful explosion than limestone. Explosive experts have to understand **geology**, the study of the Earth's structure, to work out how the rocks will break up. Splitting rock may require a series of small blasts rather than one large one.

granite   limestone

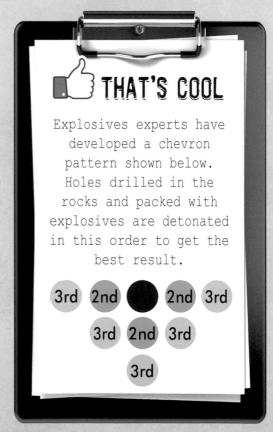

👍 THAT'S COOL

Explosives experts have developed a chevron pattern shown below. Holes drilled in the rocks and packed with explosives are detonated in this order to get the best result.

3rd 2nd ● 2nd 3rd

3rd 2nd 3rd

3rd

Bomb Disposal

Some explosives experts undertake the dangerous job of bomb disposal. Bomb disposal makes hazardous explosive devices safe. Experts either detonate explosives or remove suspected ones from public places.

There are several different ways to make a bomb safe. The method used depends on how many people are in the area. Most bombs are detonated from a safe distance, sometimes using remote controlled vehicles. Approaching a bomb is only done in emergency situations.

This remote controlled vehicle is being loaded with C-4 explosive. It will then be sent to detonate a roadside bomb. Vehicles can be fitted with cameras, microphones, sensors, or mechanical hands to open doors or handle explosives.

Bomb disposal teams use sensors that can detect sounds, odors, or images from inside a bomb. Once the technicians knows what the explosive is and what state it is in, they work out the safest way to disarm it. Preferably, this is done remotely. Sometimes technicians must put themselves at risk and make the bomb safe by hand.

FACT FILE

No suit is totally bombproof, but a blast-resistant and flame-resistant suit provides protection. The suit's tightly woven fibers help to lessen the blast. Steel or ceramic plates inside the suit help stop objects from piercing it. Padding protects the wearer from flying debris, and cushions the wearer if they are thrown to the ground. The blast-resistant helmet has a bulletproof visor, and may have headphones, a microphone, and ventilation to cool the wearer and demist the visor. A high collar protects the neck and overshoes fit over the shoes. Quick-release straps help get the suit off fast in an emergency.

A bomb disposal technician being helped into a blast-proof suit.

Film Pyrotechnics

Pyrotechnics is the use of explosive and **flammable** materials to produce special effects. Pyrotechnicians work in the film industry and help make convincing explosions, fires, and smoke effects.

Safety is vital on the film set. Pyrotechnicians need to make sure that the actors, stunt people, and everyone on the film set are safe. They need to make sure that shock waves and ground vibration from explosions don't cause structural damage to the surroundings. They need to know how to transport, store, and use explosive materials on a film set. They may advise the stunt coordinator and director on what effects can be used.

FACT FILE

The actor on the right is being fitted with small explosives called squibs. When detonated they look like a bullet has hit the actor, and the tubes gush pretend blood! The actor is wearing protective body armor under his T-shirt. Other pyrotechnic equipment includes smoke effects, maroons that make loud bangs, and small cascades of sparks that look like electrical faults.

the explosive charge

The charge is put in a steel tube and attached to a controller.

Gasoline is added to create a fireball effect.

Explosive powder is added to ignite the gasoline.

the explosion

Demolition

Some construction companies employ a full-time explosives expert. The explosives expert inspects the building and decides on the best way to demolish it.

Holes may need to be drilled and filled with explosives. The expert decides where the holes go, and how deep they should be. The main challenge is to control which way the building will fall. The easiest way to bring a building down is onto its side, like felling a tree. To topple it to the north, they detonate explosives on the north side of the building first.

FACT FILE

To demolish a building, the internal walls are taken out first. Then blasters drill holes in the concrete columns and fill them with explosives. When they explode, the sudden outward pressure shatters the concrete. For steel columns they use a powerful explosive called RDX which can slice right through the steel. The explosion is started using an electrical detonator such as a blasting cap, or by the more recently invented shock tube, which uses shock waves. To control the explosion sequence, the blasters can adjust how long it takes each explosive to go off by using timing devices.

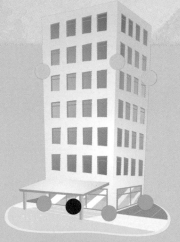

● 1st blast
● 2nd blast
○ 3rd blast

If detonated in this order, the sides of the building fall neatly into the center.

Imploding a building so it falls straight down on itself like this is not easy.

 **THAT'S COOL**

A building implosion works by blasting the support structure of a building at a precise point. The section above that point falls onto the rest of the building below. If the upper section is heavy enough it will demolish the lower section.

Sport and Entertainment

Pyrotechnic effects can make a stage show very exciting. Imagine a stage with sparks and flames lighting up every touch of a guitar string, theater action sequence, or every dancer's move.

Pyrotechnics are widely used at sporting events. Pyrotechnic devices can make smoke, noise, or sparks. The devices are usually fired by remote control. The remote control may be manual, such as a panel of switches, or it may be computer controlled.

Flame projectors help build the excitement at a Dallas Cowboys football game.

The rock band Iron Maiden use pyrotechnics in their stage act.

FACT FILE

Other popular pyrotechnics include:
Airbursts: burst into circles of sparks
Comets: shooting stars with a fiery tail
Mines: shoot out sparks, confetti, or streamers
Smoke pots: release mushroom clouds of smoke
Concussions: create loud bangs
Falls: create falling spark effects
Fireballs: project smoky rolling balls of flame
Flares: intense flames of various colors
Flash pots: create flashes, smoke, or sparks
Line rockets: whistling or colored rocket devices that travel along guide cables
Squibs: explode to look like bullet hits
Strobes: flares which flash
Wheels: spinning wheels of sparks

Confetti fired into the air by a mine.

Mines and Quarries

The mining and quarrying industry employs explosives experts. Their job is to set dynamite charges in the rock to get at the mineral or stone. They may work unusual hours so that they are not blasting while others are working.

The explosives expert, called a shot firer, is responsible for getting people to act as sentries, and putting up warning signs and barriers to stop access to the danger area. They must check the area is clear of unused explosives, and give a warning before setting the charge. After the blast, the shot firers must check the equipment is stored safely, and no misfired shots remain in the tunnel.

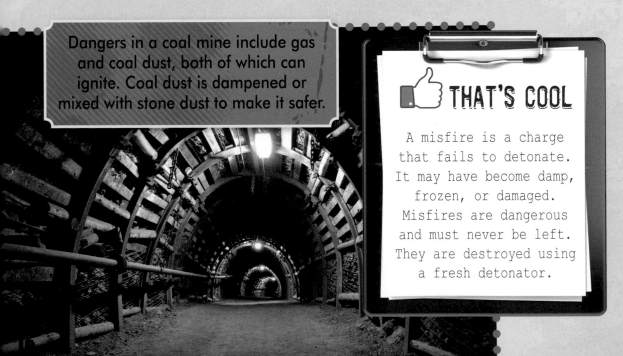

Dangers in a coal mine include gas and coal dust, both of which can ignite. Coal dust is dampened or mixed with stone dust to make it safer.

👍 THAT'S COOL

A misfire is a charge that fails to detonate. It may have become damp, frozen, or damaged. Misfires are dangerous and must never be left. They are destroyed using a fresh detonator.

Rock blasting uses different types of explosives. Higher velocity explosives are used for hard rock. Low velocity explosives are used for soft rock. The most commonly used explosives in mining today are ANFO (ammonium nitrate/fuel oil). ANFO cost less than dynamite. To use ANFO, an explosive expert drills blast holes and then tip bags of ammonium nitrate down them (left). They pour a carefully measured amount of fuel oil into the hole, too. Once a detonator is connected the explosives are ready to go.

At a quarry the explosives expert is responsible for safety in the blasting area. No one can enter that area without their permission. It is important to follow strict safety rules. For example no one may smoke, all unused explosives must be kept in a safe area, and no one can drill a hole near where someone is filling another hole with explosives.

Blasting Holes

Road and railway construction relies on explosives experts to blast their way through mountain ranges and awkward terrain. It can be a lot easier to go through a mountain than to go around it.

Drilling and blasting is still used for the construction of most tunnels. Workers sometimes use a moveable scaffold, called a jumbo, which has drills mounted on it. A number of holes are drilled into the rock. The holes are then filled with explosives. Detonating the explosive causes the rock to collapse. The rubble is removed using carts.

Some blasting cuts a channel through rock such as in the road construction pictured above. If a roof is to remain, the position and depth of the holes, the timing and the amount of explosive used are critical. The correct technique means the tunnel will have a strong arched shape that can withstand the pressure of the weight of rock above.

 THAT'S COOL

These are an explosive expert's signals:
Warning signal - a 1-minute series of long blasts 5 minutes before a blast signal
Blast signal - a series of short blasts 1 minute before the detonation
All clear signal - a long blast

FACT FILE

Below is a picture of a complicated mesh of shock tube used to blow up a rock face. The orange branch lines are attached to the yellow trunk line. A shock wave carried through the network detonates each explosive charge.

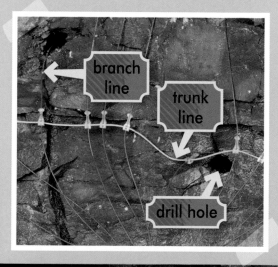

branch line

trunk line

drill hole

Arch-shaped tunnels blasted through a mountain range

Military Explosives

One of the best ways to become an explosives expert is to join the military. All military branches need people who work with explosives. Experts are used for demolition, dealing with unexploded devices, handling bomb threats, securing areas, and **mine** clearance.

When the military needs to enter a building, explosives can be the quickest way in. Pictured below, some US Marines combat engineers are practicing blowing open a door. They protect themselves against the blast using shields. Holes can be blast through some structures using just the detonation cord. They shape the cord into a man-sized shape, stick it to a wall or door with tape, and detonate it.

Military explosive experts practice their skills.

Military weapons and ammunition are called **ordnance**. Explosives experts in the military are often called ordnance technicians. Bomb disposal experts are called EOD specialists. EOD stands for explosive ordnance disposal.

A trainee explosive ordnance technician attaches a blasting cap as his instructor looks on.

FACT FILE

The ordnance disposal teams have to destroy any seized enemy ammunition. Here a US Army sergeant carefully packs the weapons' fuse holes with C-4 explosive. C-4 is a plastic explosive. It looks a little like modeling clay. It can be molded into any shape and pressed into a gap. C-4 is very stable. It can only be detonated by extreme heat together with a shock wave. It will not explode if it is dropped or even if it is shot at!

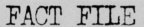

C-4 plastic explosive

How Fireworks Work

Fireworks were invented in China hundreds of years ago. There are two main types of firework, aerial and ground fireworks.

An aerial firework is usually covered in a paper casing. Inside there is a bursting charge which explodes the firework. This causes the stars in the firework to explode. The fuse acts as a time delay so the shell explodes at the right height. The firework is launched from a tube by a lifting charge of black powder. When the lifting charge fires it lights the shell's fuse.

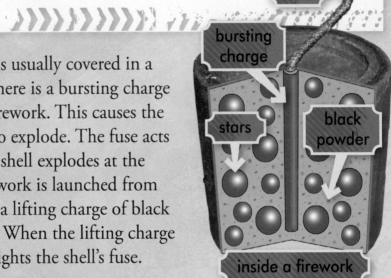

fuse

bursting charge

stars

black powder

inside a firework

Fireworks can be joined together to make a variety of sparkling shapes of different colors. Some shells contain explosives that can crackle or whistle. Ground fireworks can produce shapes such as rotating circles, stars, and globes.

China is the largest manufacturer of fireworks in the world.

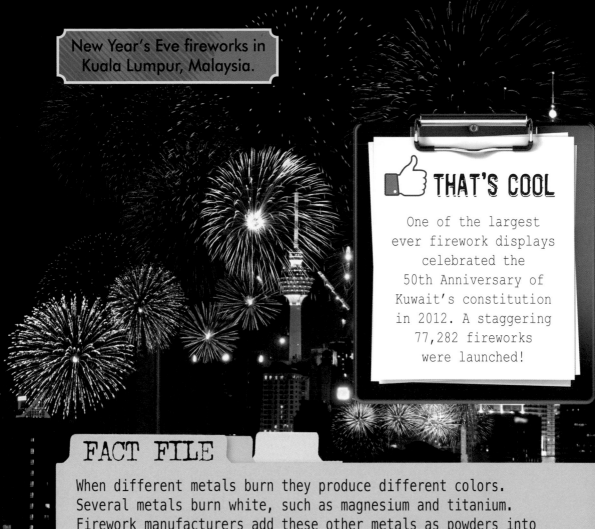

New Year's Eve fireworks in Kuala Lumpur, Malaysia.

👍 THAT'S COOL

One of the largest
ever firework displays
celebrated the
50th Anniversary of
Kuwait's constitution
in 2012. A staggering
77,282 fireworks
were launched!

FACT FILE

When different metals burn they produce different colors.
Several metals burn white, such as magnesium and titanium.
Firework manufacturers add these other metals as powders into
the firework to produce the other colors.

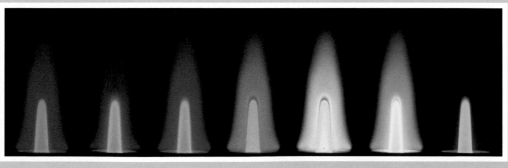

Potassium   Strontium   Lithium   Calcium   Sodium   Copper   Cesium

Fireworks Display Teams

Pyrotechnicians stage large firework displays. Fireworks are dangerous and pyrotechnicians must be fully qualified before they can give a public display.

Creating a firework display takes a lot of planning and preparation. The display director plans the show, which usually features a big opening and closing sequence. Many shows are done to music and the fireworks are planned to be in time with the music. Although display companies will keep a large stock of fireworks, some may need to be brought in specially. Crews have to be hired, transport arranged, and any special equipment needs to be built.

FACT FILE

Fireworks displays are programmed onto a computer for split-second precision. A firing box is connected to all the fireworks' fuses and plugged into the computer. When the computer says it is time to fire a certain firework an electric current runs from the firing box to a controller and then to the electric match, igniting the firework's fuse.

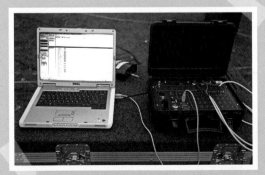

A computer (left) and a firing box (right) set up ready at a display.

mortar tubes

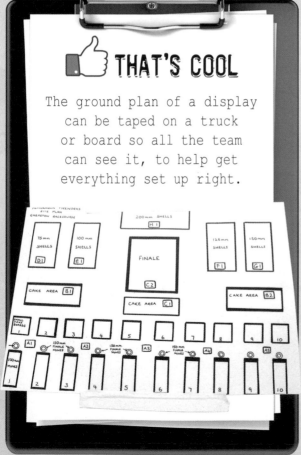

It can take days to set up a big fireworks display. When the team arrives they mark out the display area. Mortar tubes are placed in crates fixed to the ground. The fireworks are fused together into the correct sequence. Electric matches are connected to each fuse run and the firing box. When the circuits are all connected they are tested by running a tiny electric current to each match to test the connection but not actually fire it. The fireworks are covered to protect them from sparks and rain until the show is ready to go.

Transporting Explosives

Explosives experts need to transport equipment from one place to another. It is very important to do this safely.

1.4 EXPLOSIVES 1

Most countries have strict laws on how to transport explosives. Most authorities need to be told the route and when the journey will be. The vehicle must never be left unattended and is only allowed to park in certain places. No repairs can be done on the vehicle while it is carrying explosives. There are rules on the amount of explosives that can be transported, and the temperature and pressure they are stored at.

Hazard identification plates and a contact number for specialist advice usually have to be displayed on a vehicle carrying explosives.

EXPLOSIVES

Explosive containers on a truck.

Even the shoes of people transporting explosives are checked for metal studs which could produce dangerous sparks.

Most fireworks are made in China. They need to be shipped to different countries. When importing fireworks it is usually necessary to provide ingredients lists, construction details, and cross-section diagrams. Only once the authorities have classified each firework may they enter the country.

FACT FILE

Special storage boxes are used for storing and transporting explosives. Only an approved handler should have access to the keys. The boxes must be strong, usually made of steel. They must have a sparkproof lining. Explosives and detonators must be separate when stored. Specialist approved packing material is used to pack firework displays when being transported.

spark-resistant lining

explosive storage box

Still Want To Be an Explosives Expert?

To work in the explosives business, a trainee needs to decide which field to specialize in. Do they want to do firework displays, work in the military, or in demolition for example?

👍 **THAT'S COOL**

To train as a military explosives technician it is usually necessary to do military basic training and then specialize. Ordnance disposal specialists can't be **color blind**. They need to be sure what color each wire is when disarming a bomb!

The only way to become a demolition expert is learn on the job. Trainee blasters will work at an established blasting company until they have learned the job. Then, they can either stay with that company or start up their own company and compete with the blasters who trained them. Clients tend to hire a demolition company based on successful jobs it has done in the past. It's difficult for a young demolition firm to get work at first.

FACT FILE

A career as an explosives expert can be rewarding for anyone who enjoys working in a high-pressure atmosphere. It is necessary to have excellent problem-solving and planning skills to set up and set off explosives. Explosive experts need to be calm and logical. They also need to be very responsible.

To train as a fireworks pyrotechnician it is best to get hired by a display team and learn your skills on the job.

Glossary

booby trap (BOO-bee TRAP)
A concealed explosive device
set to go off when a harmless-
looking object is touched.

C-4 (SEE FOR)
A type of plastic explosive.

chemical reaction
(KEH-mih-kul ree-AK-shun)
A process that involves changes
in the structure and energy
content of chemicals.

color blind (KUL-er BLYND)
A vision deficiency that makes
it difficult to tell the difference
between some colors.

demolish (duh-MAH-lish)
To break to pieces.

detonator (deh-tuh-NAY-ter)
A device used for detonating
another explosive.

flammable (FLA-muh-bul)
Capable of being easily set on
fire and of burning rapidly.

gases (GAS-ez)
A fluid such as air that has
no fixed shape and tends to
expand without limit.

geology (jee-AH-luh-jee)
A science that deals with the
history of the earth as recorded
in rocks.

imploding
(im-PLOH-ding)
Exploding inward rather
than outward.

mine (MYN)
An explosive device placed in
the ground or water and set to
explode when disturbed.

nitroglycerin
(ny-troh-GLIS-ur-in)
An oily, explosive, and poisonous liquid used in making dynamite.

ordnance
(ORD-nants)
Military supplies including weapons and explosives.

pyrotechnicians
(py-roh-tek-NIH-shunz)
People working with pyrotechnics.

pyrotechnics
(py-roh-TEK-niks)
Fireworks used in the entertainment industry.

speed of sound
(SPEED UV SOWND)
The speed at which sound travels.

stable (STAY-bul)
Not readily changing in chemical composition or physical state.

technicians (tek-NIH-shunz)
Specialists in a technical occupation.

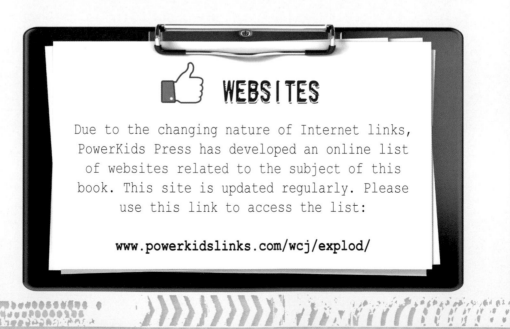

WEBSITES

Due to the changing nature of Internet links, PowerKids Press has developed an online list of websites related to the subject of this book. This site is updated regularly. Please use this link to access the list:

www.powerkidslinks.com/wcj/explod/

Read More

Gonzalez, Lissette. *Bomb Squads in Action*. Dangerous Jobs. New York: PowerKids Press, 2008.

Herbst, Judith. *The History of Weapons*. Major Inventions Through History. Minneapolis, MN: Lerner Publishing, 2006.

Oxlade, Chris. *Material Changes and Reactions*. Chemicals in Action. Portsmouth, NH: Heinemann, 2007.

Index